MW00888479

How to Be A Good Manager

Easy Ways to Become a More Effective & Higher Producing Management Professional

By
Kimberly Peters

Other Books
by Kimberly Peters

Relationship Kick Starter

How to Be a Good Employee

Table of Contents

Disclaimer

Let's get this out of the way before we get started!
Every situation is different and every person is
different as well. That being said, there is no one
perfect cookie cutter approach to everything in life
and becoming a better manager is one of those
imperfect things. Therefore, it is the responsibility of
the reader to ascertain which parts of this book, if
any, apply to his or her particular situation. The use
or application of any or all parts of this publication is
strictly the responsibility of the reader. The author,
publishers, distributors or resellers of this book are
not responsible for the use or application of any or all
the information contained in this publication.

Introduction

I'm glad you decided to at least start reading this book. Over the years I have interacted with many managers who would never even consider looking for any kind of help or guidance. And their performance and results suffered very much for that attitude. Just by being here with me on this page you have showed potential far above many other managers. So please take pride in that.

Many managers feel that they have worked hard to get to where they are in their careers and that others should be waiting in line to do their bidding or bow to their every request. We all know that type and again, because you are here you probably are not one of those types. That's good news as well.

But even more managers feel that the entire responsibility of making the manager-employee relationship work lies strictly with the employee. It is their responsibility to do a good job and it is their responsibility to make sure everything runs fine and that the results are the best they can be. Their attitude is that as long as the employee is being paid, they should do their best and if they don't, it's their fault.

Unfortunately, that attitude should have gone the way of the horse and buggy because it is no longer relevant. Both the manager and the employee have an equal responsibility in making their relationship work to the best of their ability. Only when both sides try to work together is it possible to get the best results and the best production.

In this book we will concentrate on what the boss, manager or supervisor should do in order to create the very best relationship with the people who work for them. We will discover what employees want and don't want and also the things they appreciate and find useful. By knowing this information almost everyone will be able to make subtle changes to how they approach their position. The result is usually immediate improvement in both results and employee satisfaction.

One quick thing before we get started. We know that many people who read these kinds of books do so because they feel they have an immediate problem or need that needs to be addressed now rather than later. Because of this, they usually tend to skip right to the parts of the book they feel will give them an immediate answer to their situation. While that is perfectly understandable, sometimes when you skip ahead, you do not get some of the information mentioned earlier in the book and this can limit your understanding of what you are reading now.

We developed a system that solves that problem very easily. Every chapter in this book is written as a standalone unit that can be read on its own or as part of the entire book. We will give you everything you need to understand that chapter and it will be contained within that chapter. This might require the same information to be repeated two or more times within the book.

So if you come across something you believe we already covered, it is because that same information was discussed in a different context. The great part of this process is that this is often some of the most important or valuable content and repetition allows you to remember it more clearly as well as being able to retain it for a much longer period of time.

To get the most out of this book, we suggest reading it through from start to finish. If you do need to go right to a specific part, that's just fine. But after you have done that, go back and read it from cover to cover so that you do not miss anything. Read it chapter by chapter and stop after every chapter to figure out how to apply that knowledge to your own job or situation. This makes the information "come to life" when you see it in terms that actually apply to you.

Then take the information you now possess and implement it into your daily life. You can start small by implementing just one or two strategies or concepts at a time. Work at them until they become habits and then integrate something else until that becomes habit. This is the best way to make any change successful. Slow and steady progress is much better than trying to do too much too soon and becoming burned out in the process.

This process has been shown to give you the very highest degree of success possible. Follow the process to the letter and you will see the results almost immediately!

Now, let's get started!

Communicate Well

If you were to ask employees what skills they value most in a boss or a manager, the ability to communicate effectively would rank high on the list. While some managers think all they have to do is yell or command that something be done, good managers understand the need to be able to communicate what they want and how they want it accurately and effectively.

Even the best employees can only do a good job when they know what they have to do and the way they have to do it. When this is explained to them accurately and carefully, the chances for a great result are infinitely better. It is when an employee is left to "connect the dots" so to speak that things usually go wrong.

A good manager understands that people require different amounts of direction.

|While some of your employees will be able to take a rough idea or concept and run with it, there will be others who will need to be taken by the hand and given step by step directions showing clearly what you want or expect. This does not mean these people are poor employees; they just have a different level of understanding.

Good managers also understand that confusion or misdirection costs us time and money. This cuts into productivity and can create serious budgetary problems if this behavior is not controlled and minimized. While you will never be able to foresee all possibilities or prevent all errors, quality communication can go a long way towards making things run smoother and better.

People who communicate well with other people are able to efficiently convert what is in their minds into words that accurately describe what they want. They are able to make other people understand exactly what they are talking about. Not kind of understand or think they understand but are definitely sure they understand.

There are several parts to the communication process that are very important when it comes to being a good manager. Some of the most important parts of the communication process are as follows:

Listening

You simply cannot communicate effectively if you do not listen to what others are saying. Managers need to listen to what their employees are telling them. They need to hear complaints, answer questions properly and respond to the needs of their employees. They simply cannot ignore what the employee has to say for any reason.

Not Interrupting

Not only is interrupting people rude, it also is a poor communications practice. Interrupting people is like telling people you are more important than whatever it is that you have to say. Not only that, but when you interrupt someone you are also cutting off the information they are trying to tell you and that means you are not getting all the information you might need to make a particular decision.

Speaking Clearly

If you speak too fast, too soft or are otherwise unintelligible, that means no one can really understand what you are saying. Learn to either speak up, speak at a comfortable pace, or correct whatever deficiency you might have in your delivery. In some cases a particular heavy accent can prove to be a very significant distraction.

If you are talking to a large group of people make sure to speak loudly and project your voice. Ask if everyone can hear you if you think that might be a problem. Do not wait for someone to say they can't hear you because they may never say a word to you.

Using the Right Words

Using long or impressive words when a smaller word will do is not only pretentious, it is downright confusing. Using words that not everyone understands just makes it harder for people to understand exactly what you are saying. Listening to some should be an easy and straight forward process. It should not be a challenging or difficult one. Use words that everyone understands so you are sure to get your point across to others.

Asking the Right Questions

An important part of the communication process is making sure you are being understood. The free flow of information from everyone involved is critical to the overall success of the conversation. Being able to ask the right questions to make sure people understand what you are saying helps you make certain you are being understood.

Asking questions also helps draw out areas of confusion and gives others the opportunity to respond with their own ideas and suggestions.

Managers understand that every conversation has two or more parts and that everyone has a responsibility to make sure they hear each part. Just because someone is a manager does not mean they are immune to listening to what everyone else has to say. Rank does not mean that you do not have to concern yourself with the other people. Instead, you should understand that the boss in some cases has an even greater responsibility when it comes to communications. Your rank and stature within the organization might make some people afraid to speak up and be heard.

Good managers have the ability to make people feel comfortable expressing their thoughts, ideas and concerns while maintaining the manager – employee relationship. That ability is one of the most important things a manager can possibly possess. Anything a manager can do to improve communication within his group or department will pay impressive dividends for everyone.

How Do I Do This?

Make an effort to be more specific and detailed in your requests.

Do not assume people know what you want. Tell them.

Put instructions in writing so there can be little room for misinterpretation.

Slow down when you are talking.

Pick locations that are relatively free of distractions and noises that might interfere with people hearing what you are saying.

Count to 3 after someone stops speaking before you speak. This will help you cut down on interrupting people.

Listen Well

Listening is one particular skill everyone thinks they possess even though they really don't listen well at all. Listening means much more than just hearing the words. Listening means hearing what people are saying, why they are saying it and understanding the emotions that are behind the words. If you miss any of those components, you are really not listening to everything the other person is saying to you.

One of the most dangerous attitudes a manager can possibly have is to think or believe that what their employees say is not important or relevant. The fact is what they have to say is often extremely relevant. After all, these are the people who actually perform the tasks and assignment you give them. Who better to provide input on problems or how things might be made better?

Some managers have the attitude of "been there, done that" and dismiss employee comments or suggestions. After all, they are in a position of management and might have even performed some of those same tasks on their "way up". So they know everything. At least in their minds they know everything. Often that is simply not the case..

But keep in mind that things change over the years. Procedures change, equipment changes and eventually how things are done today no longer even slightly resemble how you did them a few years ago. So the next time someone gives you a suggestion or wants to tell you about a problem, listen to them.

When we feel the input from employees is not valuable, our minds to not really pay attention. You might think you are listening but in reality, words are going in one ear and out the other. That is because you have told yourself that these words, and the information behind them, are not relevant or useful.

A good manager will tell him or herself that they can always learn something from other people. That means employees, vendors, other managers and anyone they might interact with. You never know when the next bit of valuable information is going to come along. It might be an innocent thought or idea that might be an inspiration for a dramatic change.

might indicate the start of a problem and getting it resolved now would save a ton of money and time later. As I said, you never know where this information is going to come from.

When you listen, hear more than the words. Try and hear the emotions and feelings behind them. Is the person angry, upset or frustrated with something? Knowing this is important because even if the situation is invalid, it is still influencing the attitude and feelings of the employee. As a manager, you need to be aware of how your employees feel while at work. This can dramatically influence their productivity and quality of the results they produce.

Just giving your employees the opportunity to talk about a problem or situation can make them feel better and reduce their stress. This process is called "venting" and it is an important aspect of interpersonal relations. Letting people talk also provides critical information that will help you make better and more appropriate decisions and responses.

Try and be open minded and listen to what is being said and try and figure out if it really does have merit. Give everything careful consideration. As we said, an innocent idea or thought could result in huge improvements and innovation. This is whether that thought comes from the janitor or the CEO of the company!

Taking the time and making the effort to stop what you are doing and really listening to employees is one of the skills employees appreciate and admire in management. It lets them know they are valued and appreciated. It tells them that their input is valued. You don't have to act on everything that is brought to you attention but you do need to listen to it.

How Do I Do This?

Maintain eye contact with the person who is talking.

Notice facial expressions and body language to gather more information on emotions and feelings.

Ask appropriate questions to show you are really listening.

If you are doing something else when someone is talking to you, stop doing it and focus on the conversation.

If you are really busy, make a commitment to talk to the person at a specific time in the future. For example, say "Steve, I have to get this report done in the next 15 minutes. Can we talk about this at 11AM when I can really concentrate on what you want to discuss?"

Value Others

Sometimes the little things a manager or other person does make a major difference. Just the way we interact with our employees can help them become more productive, create a more positive work environment and just help create better quality employees.

One criticism that employees frequently have regarding their managers is that they feel the manager feels superior to them and does not really value who they are and what they do. In other words, some employees feel that their manager or boss simply takes them for granted.

When a manager appears to take someone for granted and does not appear to value someone's efforts or abilities, it sends the wrong message to the employee. The manager is actually telling the employee that they are not worth very much and their contributions or efforts are not appreciated.

When this happens the employee feels marginalized and their attitude usually turns into one of apathy. Instead of wanting to do their best and perform well for their manager they have the exact opposite attitude. They think "Why bother?" because they feel that what they do and how they do it has little impact on the rest of the company. So they do less and less and care less and less along the way.

Good managers understand that making people feel appreciated and valued helps those employees feel good about themselves and what they do for the company. This attitude makes people want to do better, go the extra mile and also makes them feel that they want to improve their skills and performance.

Just taking the time to tell someone how much you appreciate them and value their performance and achievements takes only a few moments but can pay huge dividends in improving morale around the office. Managers should make it a priority to interact with their employees on a regular basis and do the little things that employees appreciate so much.

Tell your employees that they are doing a good job. Congratulate them when a project is completed on time and thank everyone for their good work.

If something goes wrong and an employee steps up and resolves the problem, don't feel that is "their job" to do that. Instead, take advantage of the opportunity to single that person out and tell them their efforts were noticed and appreciated.

Today we are all too quick to place blame or complain about the bad things. It is time we also stepped up to acknowledge good performance and success. It takes just minutes but it can pay dividends for years!

How Do I Do This?

Hold quarterly meetings with each person or in groups and go over successes and achievements and publicly acknowledge them.

Take someone aside and go over their performance and let them know you appreciate their efforts.

Bring in pizza or have lunch catered in once in a while.

Hold a contest or award a prize to someone for doing something above and beyond.

Just say "Thank You!" when someone does something for you.

Provide Feedback

Though this might seem a little contrary to popular belief, most employees want feedback on how they do their jobs and how well or poorly they are performing at that time. This information is needed and even wanted because people need to be reassured that they are doing a good job. This helps instill confidence within employees and make them more secure in the feeling that they are not in danger of losing their jobs.

Over the last few years almost every company has experienced problems, been forced to reduce headcount and take other measure to ensure their continued ability to remain in business and serve their customers.

Feedback between manager and employee is important so that everyone understands how each other feels about their performance, work ethic, attitude and other factors.

Being upfront with employees and letting them know how they are doing at certain points in the year enables people to adopt a more pro-active approach to their skills and performance.

Imagine how frustrating it might be to go to work every day and have very little idea of how your performance is thought about by others?

Imagine how it might feel to not know if you are doing great, not so great or even very poorly at your job?

Imagine how angry and frustrated you would be if you were called into the manager's office and told you were being let go because your performance was poor and you had no idea that was even a problem?

These are the things that employees in many companies experience on a daily basis. A good manager keeps his or her employees apprised of how well their performance is and what areas, if any they might consider working on. This helps the employee constantly improve their skills and abilities and make themselves more valuable to themselves and the company.

Most employees would work harder to become better if they knew that is what they needed to do. That is why feedback and performance appraisals are so important to employee attitude and performance. They are also critical for career growth as well.

At minimum a yearly performance appraisal should be done for every employee. That means sitting down with the person and going over everything that pertains to their job and career. That might include attendance, punctuality, attitude, education, performance metrics and anything else that might factor into the performance review.

While this is usually accompanied by a salary increase or review, the two need not be mutually connected. You can do this type of review with or without a salary adjustment. In fact, doing this throughout the year to give people a chance to improve themselves before salary review time might be especially appreciated!

There are other times a good manager can provide valuable feedback as well. Using everyday situations as teaching opportunities is a great way to provide positive feedback to people as they do their jobs. When someone makes a mistake, acknowledge that mistake but follow it up with constructive criticism showing that person how to do better the next time.

When we provide constant feedback to our employees we allow them to take corrective action faster and improve their skills and attitudes faster as well. We enable them to assume a pro-active role in their improvement and enable them to grow their skills and prepare themselves for a better job at the same time.

For the most beneficial result, feedback should be given on a one on one basis. That means not discussing mistakes or personal performance in a group setting. Talk to the employee in private and discuss both positive and negative things between the two of your only. This enables people to accept criticism and negative comments without feeling the need to defend themselves in front of their peers.

How Do I Do This?

Set up scheduled review periods for each employee. Yearly should be the absolute minimum with twice a year or quarterly being better.

If someone is doing an especially good job, stop by and let them know. This will not only make them feel good, they will also get an idea of what you like and will probably want to do more of that!

Hold regular staff meetings to let the group know how they are doing. Discuss projects and accomplishments and let people know when they are on the right track or when they have veered off in the wrong direction.

Handle negative criticism in a positive way by using it as a teaching experience. Everyone makes mistakes.

It matters more that they learn from those mistakes so they do not continue to make the same mistake over and over again.

Stay Calm

Business is full of pressures and stressful situation and conditions. A good manager understands this and also understands the importance of always remaining calm and under control in front of their employees. This attitude spreads to the employees and allows them to relax at the same time.

Good managers help isolate their employees from the stresses and pressures that come down from up top or from outside forces. That is one of the primary responsibilities of the manager. Making employees face the pressures of things outside of their control is counter-productive.

For example, you might be under extreme pressure to bring a project in under goal or achieve a certain financial objective. While you might have the ability to influence production or certain factors, most of your employees will not have that same ability.

In those cases you should implement whatever steps you need to take without bringing that same pressure to the employees.

The fact is, managers usually are pulled in many different directions at the same time. They might be asked to achieve different goals that are 180 degrees apart such as increasing production while cutting head count at the same time. These problems are not the problems of the employee but rather the problems of the manager. You cannot become frustrated with others and make the employees bear the brunt of those frustrations.

When management remains calm, employees see that there is no reason to panic. They also are reassured that even though things are not good at the moment, they are also not that bad either. They believe that hard work and perhaps a temporary inconvenience or two will help see things through.

When management panics, or appears to panic, that sends shockwaves down through all levels of employees in the company. Those people see people above them panic or get upset and they see the worst in things. They see things being worse than they really are. This can get employees feeling their own future becoming less secure and less bright at the same time.

A good manager will take the pressures from above and isolate their employees from those pressures as much as they can. While they might have to take certain steps or make certain changes, they do not have to make everyone worry by sharing everything with the employee.

For example, if you see sales drop for a month or so and you get pressured from above to increase sales, you have two choices. You can go to your employees and threaten them with a possible loss of job or other reactionary move or you can step back and do a little bit of research. You might already know that sales routinely go down that time of year and that things will soon be back to normal.

It that is the case you can isolate your people from that information and spare them the stress or panic. You can remain calm, weather the "storm" and wait for things to get back to normal. You could even take some pro-active steps to get sales up a little faster without panicking.

Another reason for this would be the perception of the employee. If the manager is always over reacting and panicking for the least little thing, when something really crucial comes around, the employees will not pay any attention to it. They will think this is just another over reaction to the same old manufactured crises.

Employees like a calm and level headed manager. They appreciate a manager who will calmly lay out the situation and ask for ideas or roll out their own plan for dealing with it. They like a manager who will reassure people that things will soon get better and in the meantime, here is what needs to happen.

Good managers will carefully consider how they will handle or react to any given situation. They will condition themselves to think first and react later. They will come up with plans to guide people through a problem or crises and they will ALWAYS appear I control even though at times they might not be in control at all.

Good managers will inspire confidence. Good managers are looked up to for guidance and advice. They are the voices of calm and reason when the times require it. The great part about being that kind of manager is that your employees will usually work even harder for you when you need it because they understand and respect your reactions to certain situations. This enables everyone to deal with everything in a much more productive and efficient manner.

How Do I Do This?

Think first and react second. Give yourself time to think things through.

Ask yourself if your people really need to be made aware of this. If not, keep it to yourself.

Ask yourself if the employees have any control over something. If they don't, do not burden them with it.

If something needs to be done by the employees, calmly explain the reasons and reassure everyone at the same time.

If you are about to panic, or when things get too hot, take a break to gather your thoughts and calm down before bringing it to employees.

Whenever there is a problem, try and have a solution or plan in place when you break the news. For example, say something like "We need to deal with........... but if we do.............. then everything should be fine within the next 6 months. A little reassurance goes a long way.

No matter how bad things get on the inside, always appear confident and in control on the outside. Never take out your frustrations on your employees.

Develop a team like atmosphere. Make sure you are part of any plan or action. Do not expect everyone to work harder or longer while you come in late and leave early. Share the sacrifice and play a role in everything.

Have a Little Common Sense

Here is one little thing almost anyone can do to make themselves a better manager almost immediately, Approach everything with just a little bit of common sense. Do not expect people to do more of something they are already doing to their limits. Do not expect people to do things they are not skilled or trained to do on a regular basis. In other words, be just a little bit realistic.

Though this is simple little thing to do, it is something that many managers refuse to do. They just want what they want and someone must do it whether or not it is practical to do so. That can be very frustrating to an employee.

I worked for a real winner of a manager for about 4 months. He always expected people to things that were either impossible or impractical.

He would move equipment around and not tell anyone when he did that and then yell at them when they didn't know where the equipment was. He expected people to work longer hours after cutting their salary and commissions. Then he would pick one or two people and fire them to "alert" the rest of them that they better work harder or they would get fired.

They result of this type of behavior was that he lost all credibility; people laughed at him behind his back and he lost complete control over everyone in the process. Employee after employee left for a better job with less drama and more stability.

Common sense should have dictated that making people accountable for things out of their control was counter-productive. He should have realized that when you cut salary and commissions that people were going to work less not more and that employee turnover would likely increase. He saw none of those things and the ultimate result was that the business failed and went out of business.

This does not mean you cannot challenge people to do better or to improve. But those challenges have to be achievable and possible. You might expect someone to increase sales 5% year after year but you should not expect someone to increase their sales 500% every year.

You might be able to get your staff to increase customer satisfaction by 5% but it would be unreasonable to expect a 50% improvement unless you really "sucked" with your customers the year before!

The same goes for what you expect from your employees. If you ask more or expect more of an employee, you must have a legitimate reason for doing so. You need to have valid reasons based on common sense before you assign a very aggressive goal.

You also need to think about what it is you are asking before you ask it. You need to realize that your employees are people first and employees second. Many have families and loved ones that are also part of their lives. A good manager will at least attempt to understand the implications something will have on their employees before they ask.

For example, you might have to ask someone to work an additional 20 hours of overtime one week to get a really large order out the doors. But if that were commonplace and you asked an employee with a wife and kids to work 7 days a week every week, that is another matter entirely. Money is nice but taking all the time away from family becomes more important than money.

A good manager will ask "Does this make sense to do or to ask someone to do?" They might place themselves in the place of the employee to see how they might react.

Sometimes just looking at the other point of view is enough to uncover flaws in the request that might be able to be handled better in another approach.

Another area where common sense comes into play is when the manager is asked by his or her boss to do something that just makes no sense. In those cases, the good manager will understand that it makes no sense and will come up with alternate ways of accomplishing the same thing.

Dealing with business and life with common sense helps you to become level headed and based in reality. It also helps you treat others properly and create the best overall work environment. Even though you sometimes expect less from your employees, the end result is usually that you will get more in return for treating people right.

I mean, isn't this all common sense?

How Do I Do This?

Ask yourself if something makes sense before you open your mouth.

Ask yourself what the best way to get something accomplished will be first. Then act.

Put yourself in the employee's place and determine how you would react if you were in their position.

Ask yourself if YOU could do what you are asking someone else to do. If the answer is NO, then reconsider the request.

Ask for input or suggestions on how the employees might handle something.

Always take the employee's personal life into consideration.

Have & Share a Vision

When it comes to morale and getting people on board with a project or their jobs, very few things matter as much as being able to share your vision and purpose with those who are ultimately responsible for the final product or results.

A great manager gives purpose to what their employees do. They turn a task into a goal or purpose. They add meaning and dimension to what every employee does. They make everyone feel that they are part of an important or meaningful process and that their contributions are valued and appreciated.

The reason for this is that so much of what we expect people to do these days is well removed from the final product or objective.

In some cases, employees toil away at a task without having the faintest idea why they are doing what they are doing. They see no objective or reason for what they do every day.

People have a problem doing something they see no reason or benefit for doing. Tasks without meaning or objective often receive less than a full effort and distractions and dysfunction quickly set in with most employees. Think about how you would feel after a few weeks of doing a task that you could see no benefit in doing. Would you continue to give it your best effort? Or would you soon just be "phoning in" your minimal efforts?

A good manager will make sure every employee understands what their own responsibilities mean to the overall product or objective. If their job is to put part A into part B, then the importance of doing that task right will be explained to them so they understand why it needs to be done.

When it comes to projects, goals or objectives, those should be explained as well. It is not good enough to tell someone to do something because "I told you to". A good manager realizes the benefits of having their people engaged and motivated to do their best work. People accomplish much more in far less time when they are properly motivated and focused. That is one of the most important skills of a manager.

A manager must also keep people informed of "the big picture" or their vision of where they see employees and the company in the future. They should outline opportunities, visions of growth and other factors that might make the employee more excited and committed than they were before.

That is the reason why some companies hold employee forums and "town hall" meetings on a periodic basis. They use these meeting to show their employees the results of their efforts. They want to show how far the company has grown and what growth is planned for the future as well. They do this to both thank people for their past efforts and motivate employees to do better in the upcoming months.

People respond better when they have a goal or objective. They want to see a benefit in the future for what they are doing today. Money is one form of motivation but over the long haul money fails to properly motivate some people. They want to know why they do what they do and what the results of their efforts really is.

A good manager knows the objectives of today as well as a long term vision of where they want to take things in the future. They share this vision and make everyone part of it. They show everyone their own role in this plan and get their commitment towards making their vision a reality.

How Do I Do This?

Make sure everyone knows and understands the "big picture"

Hold regular meetings to explain what is going on now and what is planned for the future.

Let others know why what they do is important. Let them know what the result would be if they did not do what they do.

When you introduce something new or different, take the time to explain why this is necessary and what the objective is for doing it.

Do your best to make employees feel that they play a vital role.

Provide encouragement to all employees and make them feel part of the team's success.

Delegate Responsibly

One of the challenges of being a great boss or manager is learning how to delegate responsibly. That means assigning tasks and workload in a responsible and efficient manner. This is frequently more difficult than most people imagine. It can be like fitting a puzzle together with the pieces being people and their different skill sets.

Good managers spread workload around so that it is balanced and appropriate. By appropriate we mean that the right person with the proper skills is assigned that particular work. For example, if you need some graphics work done you would assign that work to the person with graphics experience and skills. You would not assign that to someone with logistics background even if that person had a lighter workload at the moment.

That means assigning work to those individuals or teams that are best equipped to handle that work and get the best results in the least amount of time. This usually allows people to do what they are best at and what they enjoy the most. While employee enjoyment is not necessarily the prime consideration, it does make a lot of sense to have people do more of what they enjoy when they are at work. Let's face it, people do more and better work when they are doing something they enjoy.

Workload is another important consideration when it comes to assigning work. If you have one person overloaded with work while another is spending most of their day surfing the internet, that will create problems for not only those two people but the rest of the office as well. Things work better and more efficiently when the workload is balanced among everyone in the office. There can be times when this might not be the case but for most of the time a balanced office is a happy office.

Personalities can also play a role in work assignment as well. Sometimes managers will assign more work to one or two people because they know the work will get done on time and be done very well. They might hesitate to assign work to others who might miss a deadline or complain about the work or do a poor job.

While the goal should be to get the best results, the manager must try and be fair with everyone in the office or on the team. Just because one or two people do better work does not mean it is right for them to do the lion's share of the work. Instead, the people who do not perform at a high level should be told to improve or risk being reassigned or worse.

A prime example of this was an office I used to work in. We had 7 people in the office and we all did our jobs well except for one person who was always saying he was too overworked or busy to do all of his projects. So the manager asked the rest of us to do some of his work. While we were doing his work he was leaving early, taking long lunches and generally having a grand old time while telling the manager how hard he was working.

As you can imagine after a while what used to be a harmonious work environment turned angry and disgruntled. All because the manager failed to understand what was going on and demanded more from some employees than he did of another. The result was 6 people working harder while on lived the good life.

Sometimes the manager does all this without realizing what he is doing. Sometimes the manager might let someone do more work than the rest of the people because they want to or because they just do it without being asked.

While this is different, the dangers still apply. Whenever one or two people do more work than everyone else they risk alienating other workers and can even get burned out in the process.

With all this being considered a good manager will understand the value in assigning work in a proper and balanced manner where the skills, abilities and workload are properly distributed among everyone.

How Do I Do This?

Keep records of who was assigned what work and at what time?

Make sure skills and knowledge are properly matched with assigned tasks.

Balance the workload among everyone whenever possible.

Cross train people to be able to do more varied tasks.

Don't allow or encourage laziness.

Create an environment where people are encouraged to come to you with problems or concerns.

Don't ask people to do more than they reasonably should be asked to do on a regular basis. Doing that will likely lead to frustration and burn out.

Keep an open ear and be aware of what is happening and being said in the office so any problems or issues can be discovered with and dealt with quickly.

Setting Goals

In the same line of thought as providing feedback, establishing goals is another way of letting people know how they are performing. Goals give them targets to shoot for and enable people to create processes and procedures to help them achieve those goals and objectives.

A good manager understands that employees need specific targets or goals in order to know when they are performing at an acceptable or very good level. For example, telling your employees they have to "do better" is not a good goal.

If your boss tells you that you have to increase production by 100 pieces a day and you tell your employees they have to do better, then if they see they are now producing an extra 25 pieces a day they will think they are doing better. But they would have no idea that they are still falling short of the desired level.

A good manager understands that goals have to have certain characteristics in order to be considered "good" goals. The well known way of creating good goals is to use the S.M.A.R.T. goal system. Goals that are set with the "SMART" system possess all the needed characteristics required to create a detailed and specific goal.

A smart goal is a goal that meets the following criteria:

Specific

In order for a goal to be really useful, the goal itself has to be specific. It needs to be specific enough so that the person understands exactly what they need or want to do. "Try to increase sales goals" is not a valid goal. That is more of a desire or a focus item rather than a valid goal.

"Increase sales over the next 6 months by 22.5%" is a valid goal because it gives you a specific target to hit and a time period in which to hit it. Another example might be instead of "Improve my education" which is a desire and not a goal to "Complete my college degree by taking 3 courses each semester over the next two years". That is a valid goal because it is specific and leaves no doubt as to what needs to happen in order to achieve that particular objective.

Measureable

Goals also need to be measureable. IN other words, you need to be able to determine how close or far away you are to achieving a particular goal. Using the above example of "Increasing sales", without a specific figure in the goal you could say you increased sales if you sold 10,001 units this year instead of the 10,000 units you sold last year. That is still an increase but not a significant one. But if your goal was "Increase sales by 22%" and you so far have increased them 28% you know you are well on your way to hitting that year end goal. If you were at 5%, then you know you have to change something so you will get better results.

Specific measurements or values help us quickly determine whether we are heading in the right direction and how far we need to go to meet or exceed that goal. The more ways you can measure your performance the more accurate your overall results are going to be. For example, while "increase sales by 22% next year" is a valid goal, a more easily tracked goal might be "increase sales by 2% each month" or increase sales by 5.5% each quarter". This would allow you to easily track your monthly performance and make it easier to stay on track or make corrections.

Attainable

Goals are not very good if they are too not attainable. Whatever goal you assign to yourself, it should be something that you are capable of achieving. If a goal is assigned to you by others, they should give you the tools and resources necessary you achieve those goals.

For example, "get certified in emergency planning within the next year" is an attainable goal as long as you can afford to take the course. If this is a personal goal, you would include financial planning as part of the goal. If this was assigned to you by your company, they should pay for the courses and allocate the time for you to take them and complete the work.

On the other hand "grow 6 inches by March of next year" is not a valid goal because there is no way that you can possibly control how much your body grows, if there is any growth at all, over the next year. You can eat healthy and work out and take vitamins but your body is going to grow only as much or as little as your gene tell it to grow.

Realistic

Though this can sometimes be similar to attainable, any goal that you assign yourself, or that is assigned to you, should be attainable.

It should be based in reality and take into consideration all the relevant factors that might influence that goal.

For example, "grow sales by 10%" might be a realistic goal in many cases. But if you were assigned the goal of "increase sales 4,000% next year" is most likely not an achievable goal. "Lose 10 pounds over the next 6 months" is an achievable goal for most of us. "Lose 100 pounds by next month" most certainly is not!

If your goal is realistic you can keep motivated to work towards it for longer period of time. If it is unrealistic then most of us will just look at it and not even bother to get started on it. Unrealistic goals just set up people for failure.

Timely

Dates and time frames are usually what separate goals from desires or hopes. If we have a goal with no stated time frame or deadline, then it is impossible to know whether we are on schedule or not. For example, "lose 10 pounds" might be a goal but what if you took 40 years to lose those 10 pounds? Does that mean you achieved your goal? Technically yes but that was not what you probably had in mind when you stated you wanted to lose weight. A better goal would be "Lose 10 pounds within the next 6 months." That gives you a time frame by which you can track your progress.

You should ALWAYS assign a time frame to your goals. This helps you get and stay motivated while giving you a much higher chance of completing things on schedule.

Creating goals using this system helps ensure that you and your employees will always be on the same page as far as expectations and performance are concerned. Good managers create detailed and achievable goals. They do not have outlandish expectations when it comes to time required to achieve the particular goal or the size of the goal itself. Good managers create goals that both meet the needs of the company while at the same time remain achievable for the people involved.

In some cases a good manager might feel the need or desire to see how much an employee or group of employees are capable of achieving. IN those cases the manager might assign a SMART goal but also include a "stretch goal" designed to challenge people to achieve even more.

Stretch goals are usually slightly higher than the standard goal and sometimes have an incentive or reward attached to them. For example, you need to produce 100 more of a product every month to hit your goal. But your stretch goal might be producing 125 more products. If the group achieves that goal everyone gets a gift card or a lunch is catered in for everyone as a reward.

Stretch goals are not required and are not always a good idea. But when used correctly, you can get more production from people on a time limited basis. But always keep in mind that stretch goals, like regular goals, must always be achievable.

How Do I Do This?

Make it a priority to always use the SMART system when creating and assigning goals.

Break down large goals into smaller goals to help keep people motivated. For example, instead of a yearly goal, break it down into 4 quarterly goals. These smaller goals are usually not as intimidating.

Always make every goal achievable. If you assign outrageous goals many people will not even attempt to achieve them.

Congratulate people when they achieve a goal. Positive feedback and acknowledgement is a powerful motivational tool.

Take your management goals and create employee goals that "roll up" into your goals. So when your people achieve their goals, you automatically achieve some of yours. Never set an employee goal lower than your own. If you do that you are setting yourself up for failure.

Hold regular meetings with employees to discuss their progress towards their goals. This gives the employee feedback and gives them an advance chance to alter their approach to help them get back on track.

Motivation

One area that usually separates really good managers from the rest of the pack is motivation. It is amazing what some manager's feel represents motivation when it comes to employees. But the fact remains that proper motivation, when used correctly, can increase both production and morale at the same time.

By definition, motivation means anything that is done to improve performance, production, attitude, or the quality of the results. More simply put, motivation means doing something to help someone want to do a better job or put forth a better effort. Motivation makes people WANT to do better.

Motivation should not be confused with fear or forcing people to do more or produce better results.

That is one area where some deluded managers lose their focus. You cannot motivate people using force or fear for long periods of time. That approach might work for a short time, and it might only work once or twice but eventually employees will become immune to such tactics and either resist or leave for another job.

I had used the example of a manager I worked for who used to fire two people every 6 months to "motivate" everyone else into working harder. This not only did not work, it became sort of an office joke with people betting on who would be next. Really good performers usually left for other jobs where they didn't have to put up with that type of behavior. The company eventually went out of business. Good strategy!

Another form of motivation is used by an amazing number of managers. I say amazing because this is the most ridiculous, even downright stupid, form of motivation I ever heard. Yet I personally have had several managers use it on their staff.

The form of motivation I am referring to is telling people if they do well, they "will still have a job to come to every day". Or perhaps they will use the even condescending "just be thankful you have a job to come to every day".

When a manager tells an employee this they are in fact telling them they are almost worthless and they should be thankful that the company even bothers continuing to pay them to work there.

This is condescending and rude and employees remember this. This form of motivation is counter-productive and once people find other jobs they will usually leave, often without notice, and move on. At the very least their attitude will change dramatically for the worse and the result of this "motivation" is usually lower productivity and production.

The reason most managers' use this is because in certain economic times, when the company may have a huge advantage of over its employees, this might temporarily work. But the damage will have already been done and when opportunities become available in the future, high turnover is usually the result.

Instead, motivation is most always a positive force in the workplace. That means providing some kind of positive event or reward for achieving a goal or accomplishing an objective. Our minds react to positive things with excitement and fulfillment. Sometimes just the thought or a positive experience at the end of the goal is enough to keep people motivated and focused.

One common misconception is that motivation must always revolve around money or financial compensation. The most common forms of bonuses are stock options, bonus payments, gift cards and other similar payments. In this type of motivation the employee sees a financial reward at the end of the task. They create their own personal motivation based on whatever suits them.

For example, if you give someone $500 for reaching a goal. For one employee that might mean he gets his new flat screen television he wants. For another employee, it might mean a new dress or pair of shoes. For someone else it might mean paying down a credit card debt or loan. Whatever the money is used for, it motivates that individual in a certain, more personal manner.

Another misconception is that a salary increase should serve as a permanent motivator for all employees. The feeling is that if I give you an increase now, it should motivate you for right now and for years to come. That is false because once someone "gets used" to the money it stops becoming a motivating factor.

While you feel great when you get the first check or two with the increase in it, after a while you just see the check and not the increase. It becomes something that is expected and not appreciated like it once was.

The novelty of the larger check has worn off and now people react to and expect now from that point on. It's not that they no longer like the money; it has just lost its motivational impact.

In order for motivation to work it has to be implemented properly. It should always be done with a positive intent and the manager must be careful not to overuse it and risk the process losing its effectiveness. But a good manager will understand the value of properly using motivation in order to keep their employees focused and committed to giving their best effort.

How Do I Do This?

Offer a bonus or reward for the top performer.

Offer a sales quota bonus for exceeding sales projections.

Bring in lunch when a department achieves a goal or lands a big contract.

Give out Certificates of Achievement when someone does a good job!

Give an employee a "free" day off for exceptional performance

Hold an "Awards Night" or lunch where bonuses and awards are given out in front of other employees.

Publicly recognize good performance.

Create an "Employee of the Month" award with a prime parking spot as the prize. Put the employee's picture in a frame on the wall for that month.

Give high performing employees a jacket or a hat signifying their performance.

Find any way to recognize achievement that might motivate any employee!

Learn from Your Mistakes!

Everybody makes mistakes and there is no way to go through life without making more of them. No matter how smart you are or how experienced you are, there will always be something you missed or failed to consider. Adding to that, there will always be something that doesn't go according to plan or react the way you though it would.

So the issue is not how to stop mistakes but what you do once you make them. There are three ways you can go when you make a mistake. You can cover it up, refuse to acknowledge it or you can take responsibility for your mistake, learn from it and move on.

It astounds me the number of people who go through life using the first two approaches to handling their mistakes. They either ignore them or try and cover them up and go on as if nothing happened. Oh, wait, there is a fourth thing you can do as well and many bad managers do this too. They blame their mistakes on other people.

If you quickly want to become known as a really bad manager, then blame everyone else for your mistakes and cover up the ones that you can't blame others for. Don't take responsibility for anything that doesn't work out well for you. But be sure to grab all the credit when things go great!

You might laugh at that last paragraph but you would be amazed at the number of managers and bosses who do just that. They are so afraid of looking weak or incompetent that they look for anyone else they could possible blame for what they have done. They might do it to their face, which makes it even worse, but they will tell others all about it. They might tell their boss, "Well, I told Bob this was a foolish way to cut costs but I guess he didn't listen. I will go fire him now."

A good manager will go to great lengths to accept responsibility for not only their actions but sometimes even for the others of others as well.

A good manager understands the value of creating a culture and environment where people are encouraged to try new things and take the initiative whenever they feel the need to do so. This kind of environment does create the possibility of making more mistakes but it also allows creativity and innovation to thrive at the same time.

If "Bob" made an honest mistake that didn't work out that well, the good boss might say something like "I thought that was a good idea and I was surprised as anyone when it didn't work. But we have talked it through and make the necessary adjustments to make sure this never happens again." IN this example the manager acknowledged the mistake, took responsibility for it and did not mention "Bob" specifically.

Do you think "Bob would respect and appreciate that? Do you think "Bob" would think highly of his manager and be more willing to work harder for him? Even more important, do you think "Bob" might not be as hesitant to try something different next time? He might be a little more careful but he would not be afraid.

Every good manager understands that people will make mistakes. It is part of life. But if you can take that mistake and turn it into a learning experience where the person, or perhaps even others, will learn from that experience and grow, then everyone winds.

The only thing worse than making a mistake is making that same mistake over and over again in the future.

That's exactly what happens when we do not take responsibility for our actions or mistakes. When we suffer no consequences, we don't really learn from that mistake. We are far more likely to make that same mistake again in the future. But if we accept the mistake, if we take the responsibility for it and accept the consequences, we will learn from the mistake and grow as a manager.

So if you make a mistake, admit it, own it and learn from it. If it impacts other people, apologize for it and do whatever you can to lessen the impact. Your employees do not see you as perfect and they don't expect perfection from you. What they do expect you to do is what you expect from everyone else. To take responsibility for your actions and decisions and learn from them.

How Do I Do This?

If you make a mistake, admit it and take responsibility for it.

After you make the mistake, take the time to go over it, analyze it and figure out where you went wrong. This will help you understand what needs to be done better or differently in the future.

If a mistake came from lack of knowledge, improve your knowledge, or find someone who knows more about that particular situation and consult them in the future.

If someone makes an honest mistake, take the time to explain where things went wrong and how things should be done in the future. Do it in a positive manner and do not be confrontational. You want to retain the positive workplace atmosphere.

When things to go wrong, or when they go in another direction that catches you unaware, consider a group meeting to discuss this so everyone understands what happened and why. Do not use specific names or place blame, just discuss the situation so that everyone else might learn from it.

If the same, or similar, mistakes are made in the future, consider implementing safeguards to further limit future occurrences of the same mistake.

Lead by Example

A whole bunch of people reading this chapter are going to think that I have gone crazy or lost my head. Because what I am going to ask you in this chapter is going to really challenge some of you. In this chapter we are going to talk about the importance of leading not by your voice but by the example you set in front of your employees.

There appears to be a disease running through management all over the world. This disease can be referred to as "Management Disconnect Syndrome". Managers suffering from this disease hold themselves above the employees and do not practice the same values or approaches to work that they expect of their employees. The problem with this disease is that it appears to be spread from manager to manager within the company.

A good manager understands the need to connect with their employees and set the proper example for them to follow. After all, you cannot expect employees to respond to a manager asking them to work hard when they see him goofing off all day long. If the manager comes out of his office and yells at everyone to work harder and produce more and then heads out for a 3 hour lunch, their credibility will plummet.

A good manager will not let their status or position within the company keep them from rolling up their sleeves and pitching in when the situation requires it. If a crises occurs and the manager is there becoming part of the solution, the employee see that and appreciate it. They see the manager as not just a figurehead who sits in the office all day long but as someone who is willing to step in and help when needed.

A good manager figures out what they want to see in their employees and creates the same example in how they portray themselves at work. If they do not want to manage a bunch of clock watchers, they should arrive early and stay late to set the right example. If they want people to become free thinkers and innovators, then they too must adopt that approach.

Just like parents set the proper examples for their children, so must the manager set the right example for their employees.

They must behave like the employee should behave. If the manager wants to have a businesslike and professional environment, they have to act that way as well. If they demand everyone wear a suit and tie, then they should wear a suit and tie.

Managing using the philosophy of "do what I say and not what I do" does not work well at the office or in the rest of your life. Many people do not grasp one simple concept. That concept is that we teach people how to treat us in life. We teach people by acting in the same manner we want others to act when they are with us. You cannot be disrespectful and expect others to treat you with respect at the same time. You need to carry yourself in the same manner you want others to carry themselves.

The same goes for attitudes as well. If you want employees to remain calm when problems occur then you must remain calm as well. If you overreact to everything that happens then eventually they will react that way as well. If you act in a different way than you expect others to react, then that creates confusion over what is right and what is wrong.

If you are in the position to dictate what the work environment is going to be, then it is only fair that you are in the position to influence it as well.

So when someone does something that you don't particularly like, or when the work environment is not like you want it to be, then look at yourself first and see if you are part of the problem or part of the solution.

How Do I Do This?

Look inside yourself first to see if you are acting in the manner you want others to act. If you are not, then force yourself to change.

If you need to change a certain behavior in others, change it within you first and then set the right example.

Understand what you expect from your employees and then expect that from yourself.

Don't expect someone to act in a way that you are not willing to act yourself.

Hold yourself to a higher standard than you hold your employees.

Grow Your Employees

If you take a look at the people who are considered really good managers, you will see that they excel in two different areas. First, they develop a reputation for being able to get things done and achieve their goals. But the second are in which they excel sometimes gets overlooked by everyone except the employees. That area is developing the skills and abilities of their employees.

Employee development is an important role of the manager. It is up to the manager to evaluate the skills of each employee and put those skills to the best use possible. They are also charged with encouraging employees to improve those skills by whatever means available. That might mean giving certain people more responsibilities, approving classes and seminars, or providing on the job mentoring.

Many of the better jobs today are filled from within using employees whose skills are already known and recognized. This is often better than bringing someone in from the outside and hoping their skills are as advertised.

Because of this, one of the responsibilities of a good manager is to discover the better employees and prepare them for the next phase of their career. That means letting them know the opportunities available to each employee and informing them what each opportunity entails and what is required to take advantage of it.

The result of this counseling and process should be to prepare people for the next phase of their career. That means making sure everyone has the skills, education and experience to move on to the next level whenever possible. The manager's goal should be to have as many employees move up the corporate ladder as possible.

Now some managers do not believe in this because it makes the manager's life much more difficult. Managers like good employees and some of them go to great lengths to keep them. While this is understandable, a good manager will not stand in the way of any employee trying to better themselves. Instead, a good manager will encourage that and take pleasure in watching their employees rise to the top.

This should be part of every employee review or evaluation. Every employee should be asked where they see themselves 5 year or so from now. The manager should understand what the employee wants and then should figure out what they can do to help make that happen. This helps keep employees happy and motivated.

From the employee's perspective, a manager interested in their career and personal growth indicates a manager that cares about them not only as a worker but as a person as well. This makes the employee think more positively about both their manager and the company they work for.

This also helps motivate the employee to do better work and improve over time because they see the benefit of doing so in future opportunities and advancement. Since this is a topic of discussion at performance reviews and evaluations, it keeps the employee focused on doing a good job while preparing for the future.

From the company's perspective, the manager who constantly produces higher quality employees to take advanced jobs speaks very well not only for the employees themselves but also for the manager who lead them to be more productive and more valuable.

In business we have something called a win-win situation where both parties get something out of a solution or action.

IN this case, when a manager motivates and prepares an employee for a better and brighter future, both the manager and employee both "win".

How Do I Do This?

Ask your employees where they see their next career step.

Look at every employee and discover their strong points. Then match those points with appropriate jobs.

Use performance reviews and appraisals to keep employees focused on self-improvement and a brighter future.

Encourage employees to take courses or attend seminars and trade conferences whenever possible. Offer to pay for some of these if the budget allows.

Make it easy to improve knowledge. Bring in consultants or hold meetings where skills are taught in-house. Making things more convenient will help everyone improve.

Have employees fill out a career plan with specific objectives to be achieved in the upcoming year.

Make it mandatory for an employee to do something every year to improve their skills or knowledge.

Use work situations to pass on your knowledge and expertise to others. This can especially apply to management skills.

To Be or Not to Be.........

This section of the book deals with the particular traits that employees appreciate in their bosses or managers. These are the qualities that inspire people and provide them with everything they need from management.

This is not to say that you have to be all of these things but you should at least try! The more you can bring these traits and qualities into your management profile the easier you will find it to create a better and more productive workplace environment.

Read through these equalities and pick one or two you think would benefit you and then implement them into your life and management style. When those become habit and no longer require your efforts, then move on to one or two ore until you have hit all the ones you wanted to target.

This is probably not going to be all that difficult. After reading through these traits you will usually see that you already posses some, if not most, of these traits and characteristics. But be honest with yourself when it comes to deciding if you need "work" on anything. Don't convince yourself you are good at something that you are not. You are only fooling yourself and hurting yourself and your employees!

Are you ready? Then let's get started!

Be Fair

When it comes to being a good manager, one of the most important things is to be fair with all your employees. While no reasonable person expects perfection from another person, most people expect to be treated in a fair and equitable manner.

As a manager, you have a responsibility to all your employees not just one or two favorites. A good manager understands that they cannot treat one person better or worse than everyone else unless there is a really good reason for doing so. Even then, treating anyone unfairly is not a good practice.

All managers have people they like better than others. These employees might be the ones who perform at a higher level, have been with the company longer, or just people that you have a higher comfort level with. Whatever the reason, in every office there are employees the manager likes more than others.

But that does not mean that those employees should get to play by different rules. A well run office has established rules and procedures that MUST be followed by everyone. You cannot make one or two people exempt from the rules and expect everyone else to adhere to them. Not only doesn't that work, it will create resentment and other problems within the office.

For example, if your office starts their workday at 8 AM and you allow Bob to come in at 8:30 almost every day, other people are going to want to come in at 8:30 as well. If you tell them they can't do that, they will ask why Bob gets to come in late and they don't. This brings your credibility as a manager into doubt.

If you have established rules and procedures in your office, make sure they apply to everyone. If there is a good reason to make an exception for someone, such as a specific office need or a personal issue with one employee that necessitates a change, then be prepared to explain that to the other employees.

For example, if Bob was in a car accident and his car will be in the shop for a month, you might allow Bob to come in at 8:30 instead of 8AM so that his wife can drop him off on her way to work because they only have one car.

IN this case that would still be treating people fairly while still showing some compassion. That is totally different than letting Bob come in an hour late because you like Bob.

It is also important to treat everyone the same because there might be legal implications if you don't. If you let the guys take longer lunches but not the women, that is against the law. If you allow some employees extra days off, that might violate employment rules as well. This is no small matter when it comes to lawsuits and reported labor law violations.

How Do I Do This?

Quite simply, do not make exceptions based on personal feelings or whom you like or dislike. Treat everyone fairly and equitably.

Do not create a different set of rules for just one or two employees unless there are valid reasons for doing so.

If you do allow someone to do something different than other employees are allowed to do make sure you have a good reason for doing so and that it does not violate any labor laws or company policy.

Keep business and personal lives separate to avoid conflict of interest.

Be Consistent

Being consistent can be one of the easiest and toughest things for a manager to do. Even though all situations are different, a good manager understands the need to behave in a responsible and consistent manner. This helps create stability within the office and also helps provide a clear understanding of what people should do in different situations.

Most employees crave some sort of stability. They want to understand what they are to do in a certain situation so when that situation arrives, they are fairly confident that they are doing the right thing. No one likes to make mistakes and most people, when given the right training and instruction, will prefer to choose the right path. But if that path is unclear, or whenever people become confused, things just don't run smoothly.

For example, if a customer returns a product one week past the return period and someone gives that customer a refund, You might tell that person that what they did was wrong and to never do that again. But if the next time someone comes in and asks for a refund when they are one week past the return period, you must react the same way. You cannot tell the person they should have given that customer a refund. If you do that the employee now has no idea what to do when the next customer comes in with a similar request.

If someone asks for a vacation day after a holiday and you tell them that is against company policy, you should not tell the next employee who asks for the same thing that their request is approved. You either enforce the rules and policies to handle these situations or you don't. You cannot have it both ways and still have stability in the workplace.

Now that does not mean that exceptions cannot or should not be made. Every situation is different and there might be valid reasons for doing something different or opposite what is normally done. For example, one of those customers who is requesting a refund a week after the return period might have had a lot of problems with that product before and you are granting the refund because it was the right thing to do.

Whenever there is a valid reason for doing something different or reacting different it is all right to do that as long as you explain to the people involved why you are making that decision. As a manager you have the right and authority to make those kinds of decisions but you should explain the reasons behind them to keep things running smoothly.

A good manager understands that rules and guidelines enable people to do more things without asking for guidance or permission. This helps things get done faster and helps everything run smoother and more efficiently. So when someone makes a mistake, or handles something in the wrong manner, take time to explain why what they did was wrong so they will know better next time and make the right decisions moving forward.

How Do I Do This?

First of all, know and follow all the rules, regulations, policies and procedures. When you consistently enforce those, you create stability in the workplace.

Know the reasons behind the rules or policies. They were created to address a particular need and understanding that need can make things much clearer.

Ask yourself "What do the rules say and did this employee follow the rules?" Just answering that question will help you act correctly 99% of the time.

Whenever you feel it is proper or necessary to act outside of the rules, explain why to the people involved. This will enable them to understand why things should be handled on an exception basis and will help keep the rules intact.

Be Confident

Being a good manager is often a thankless job and you find yourself being pulled or torn in several directions all at the same time. At times you might feel your patience and skills are being tested and you are not sure how to handle things. At those times a good manager knows the importance of remaining confident in his or her abilities.

Acting with confidence inspires confidence in the eyes of your employees. When they see their manage acting with confidence, they become reassured that you know what you are doing and that you know the best way of getting something done. Employees will follow the instructions and direction of a confident manager much more easily than one they feel is unsure of what they are doing.

Managers need to have the support of their employees in order to help get things done faster and with better results.

Often times a task or assignment will need to be done that the employees either do not want to do or fail to see the need for doing it in the first place. Even after having the need explained to them they might be inclined to not support it if they have little faith in their manager.

Confidence also helps resolve disputes or disagreements as well. If there is more than one answer to a problem or situation, there can be differences of opinion as to which is the right way to proceed. If the employees are confident in their manager, they will be more likely to support the direction the manager wishes to go.

This is important because it is the responsibility of the manager to lead their employees. The manager is the one who is responsible for making sure that things get done in a specific manner and within a specific deadline. Since the manager is the one responsible, they are the ones who make the final decisions. The manager then needs to have the respect of their employees to support that decision.

Acting confident also reassures the employees and reduces stress at the same time. When you have a leader who is strong and acts strong, you develop a feeling of confidence in that person. Since every workplace has some degree of uncertainty in it, being confident in your boss or manager makes things feel more secure and less stressful.

How Do I Do This?

Know your abilities. Confidence comes from knowing who you are and what you are capable of. Experience helps give you confidence because once you have done something; you know you are capable of doing it again.

Understand the situation. The more you understand something, the less you become unsure about. Doubts come from uncertainty so removing uncertainty removes doubts.

Get help when you need it. If you aren't sure about something, ask someone for help. Getting someone else's guidance or assistance can help you feel more secure and confident.

Act with confidence on the outside even when you have doubts on the inside.

Make informed decisions. The more information you have before making the decision the more confident you will be that it is the correct decision.

Don't act first and think second unless it is absolutely critical that you do so.

Rely on your experience. The best predictor of what is going to happen is what has happened before in similar situations.

Be Reliable

Employees like people who are reliable. They want their co-workers to be reliable and they expect their manager or boss to be reliable as well. After all, if you cannot rely on your manager to do the things that they should, who can employees really count on?

Business today is chocked full of managers who seem to always be too busy to take care of the things they should. They are too busy attending meetings to make sure the office is running properly. They are too busy taking phone calls to do the work or task that they promised people they would do last week. These managers all seem too busy to do the most important part of a manager's job.

That part of their job is making sure the office or work environment is running smoothly and that all problems and issues are being addressed.

That mean be available to do what needs to be done to address issues, fulfill commitments and take care of employee and work related issues.

That means if a manager commits to perform a certain task or take care of something then they need to follow through on that commitment. For example, if performance reviews are expected to be completed by a certain date, then the manager should make it a priority to see that they are completed within that time frame. The manager should not put them off, and possibly delay a salary increase, until they feel it's "convenient".

Far too often employee needs or issues are put off or simply disregarded by the manager. This is almost the same as telling someone that their needs or priorities are of little value to the company. In essence the manager is the employee's connection to the company. If that connection proves to be unreliable, the attitude of the employee, and the relationship with the company, is likely to suffer.

If a manager tells an employee that they will do something, then the manager must make every effort to come through with that promise. If, for some reason, that becomes impossible for certain reasons, the manager must explain those reasons to the employee. Even in those cases, the manager must make every effort to try and come through even though certain obstacles might now exist.

The ability for the employee to believe in the words of the manager is the core of the employee / manager dynamic. It needs to be a two sided relationship. The manager must believe in the employee and the employee must believe in the manager. When this is intact, both employee and manager continue to trust and believe in each other. Once that trust is broken, or a commitment is not fulfilled, the relationship becomes damaged.

Think about how important it is in your life to truly feel you can rely on someone. You almost always feel that way about your spouse, your friends and valued associates. If you value that feeling in your relationships with others, don't you think your employees are likely to feel the same way?

How Do I Do This?

It's really simple!

If you say you will do something, then do it.

If something has a deadline, then meet that deadline.

If you are needed by your employees, be there for them.

If your employees need support, provide support.

Simply treat employee need in the same manner you would like them to treat yours.

Be Specific

If you ask employees if they would prefer detailed instructions or just to be given generic details and be told to "run with it", most employees would prefer to receive detailed instructions. This is because detailed instructions allow the employee to more fully understand what their manager wants and how they should go about accomplishing it. It leaves much less to chance that mistakes will be made.

Some managers believe that what they want is pretty straight forward and that there should be little to discuss because of that. While this might be true for some tasks, or when a task is a recurring one that people are accustomed to, providing specific and comprehensive details or information usually helps the employee to a better and more accurate job.

Simple tasks might be able to be described simply such as "Throw this away in the recycling container". You shouldn't have to say "Take this 8X11 piece of paper and insert it into the blue trash container on the left hand side of the office wall with the recycling logo in white on the front". "Throw this out should be sufficient. Maybe you can tell a new employee where the container is if it is hidden but everything else is pretty obvious.

But let's say you have to have someone write a report and that this report has to contain data or information obtained at a specific time. If you do not provide specific instructions about the data needed, how to go about getting the data, and when the data should be gathered, then the accuracy and quality of the report may suffer.

For example, let's say you have a quarterly report due next week and you assign one of the employees to do that report for you. It's not that difficult but it has to be done right. Now you might say "Bob, here is the report form, and here is the data required. Please give this to me by next Tuesday." Bob understands what for he is supposed to use and what data is needed and when it is due. But he knows little else and some of what he doesn't know might hurt his abilities to produce an accurate report.

But what if the manager said this to Bob?

"Bob, I need the quarterly report done by next Tuesday. It is not difficult and here is the form you should use when preparing the report. Here is a list of the data you will need as well as the name of the reports you will find that data in on our servers. Be sure not to run these reports until Monday morning as all our data is uploaded and refreshed on Fridays. Waiting until Monday will give you the most accurate and up to date results. Section one is where you write your summary of sales activities and explain anything that might have had an impact on sales this quarter. Don't forget the blizzard we had that caused us to close 3 stores for a week. That definitely had an impact on our sales. The last part is for future forecasts. Make sure to mention the Expo we will be at in May. Any questions?"

While that might seem to be a lot to say, it takes less than a few minutes to say that and it provides critical information that Bob can use to do his report properly and accurately. Just knowing that the data report have to be run on Monday was of huge importance. Maybe Bob might try and impress his manager and get the report done early. So he runs the reports on Thursday and misses an entire week of sales. He would then produce an inaccurate report and possibly might have to do the report all over again. That is if anyone noticed before it was too late!

Many times the difference between good and great lies in the details. Details turn a generic request into a specific one. Detail give clear and accurate direction and gives you a much better chance of getting what you want, when you want it and how you want it. It is like playing "connect the dots". You give everyone all the direction and information they need to do their best. This results in fewer mistakes, less lost time and fewer resources required to get the job done.

For the employee, detailed instructions allow this to relax and more fully understand what the manager really wants. In the example above the manager ended the discussion by asking any questions. This allowed the employee to further clarify anything they were not sure of. If detailed instructions were given to the employee there usually would be fewer questions at the end of the discussion.

When people are more specific about what they need or are asking for, the result is also a far less stressful work environment. People know what they are expected to do and how they should go about it. There is less guesswork and far less frustration.

Another benefit, or also possibly even a negative, is accountability. The more specific you are about things, the more ownership you take for the outcome. The more detailed your instructions, the more responsible you are for the end result.

That is exactly why so many managers provide as little direction as possible. That is so they can distance themselves from a bad result and blame others!

But since we do not have to concern ourselves with trying to escape responsibility, let's make an effort from this point forward to become more specific and detailed in our requests and instructions. You don't have to be obnoxious about it, just be thorough and detailed.

How Do I Do This?

Don't assume that someone knows what you want and how you want it. Tell them.

Don't rush through the instructions. An extra minute or two now can save hours or even days later!

Think about what might possibly be confusing and make it more detailed and specific.

Think about where something is likely to go wrong and then provide more details about that area of the request.

Think about what questions might come up and answer them in the instructions before the question is even asked.

If this is a repeat request that many people might be involved in, consider putting instructions in writing. This will save you from repeating this over and over and give everyone a "template" to use so that everyone does the task the same way.

Be a Team Player

While there needs to be a separation between manager and employee, there cannot be such a separation that the manager is not thought of as "part of the team". The manager is a critical part of the team and in many ways is the team leader. It is when the manager distances himself from the rest of the team that problems occur.

Some managers consider themselves "team players" because they feel the team is there to do his wishes and to turn every whim into a reality. This is a dangerous precedent to set as it often alienates most employees against the manager.

Most good managers understand that their function is not only to lead their employees down the right path but to also become part of their success

. In other words, they not only lead, they participate. When the manager becomes an active member of the team, everything runs better. Everyone becomes more engaged and more committed. But if the manager assumes the role of dictator and tyrant, things quickly go off track.

In a team environment, the traditional manager / employee dynamic is usually cast aside. In the team environment every member of the team has an input and influence on how things are done. While there is a leader on the team, that leader is more of a moderator instead of someone who dictates or rules with a heavy hand.

Perhaps a better representation of a manager being a team player would be the manager assuming the role of a mentor rather than a boss. A mentor provides direction and leadership while still allowing the employee to learn, grow and play an active role in how things are done. In this dynamic the manager empowers the employee to do more, accept more responsibility and to play a more active role in the team.

Offices and companies work better and are more productive when the manager is more of a leader and mentor than when they behave in more of a dictatorial capacity. When managers are equally concerned with their employee's growth and needs as they are with their own, everyone wins.

Employees become more engaged and motivated. Managers become more successful as their employees are willing to work harder and longer for them.

Two of the primary roadblocks to becoming a team player are the manager's ego and their insecurity. Being a team player means sacrificing individual rewards, recognition and glory and transferring those things to the team. That means the team shares the rewards and recognition not the individual. This can be difficult for some people to do and sometimes it takes a lot of concentration and commitment especially at the beginning.

Insecurity plays a significant role in becoming a team player as well. Insecure people are usually hesitant to give up control or recognition to others. They feel a need to take all the credit in order to appear better in the eyes of others. Secure and confident people, on the other hand, do not feel that way and are far more likely to thrive in a team environment.

Good managers lead by example and allow their employees to do their job in the best way possible. They are there for guidance and support whenever it is needed but they take a back seat role. Good managers give the credit to their team and do not take it all for themselves.

This is important because the overall success or failure of the team becomes the success or failure of the manager. It is far better for the manager to become known as a great leader than it is to achieve a goal or two all by themselves.

How Do I Do This?

Be a leader and not a dictator.

Look for ways to get employers more engaged and motivated.

Be a resource for those employees who need it.

Be quick to give credit to the team rather than to yourself.

Develop a team mentality where everyone is encouraged to participate in process and policies.

Place the needs of the team above your own wherever possible.

Be Respectful

Being respectful to others is something that should be very basic and automatic for everyone. Unfortunately, for a lot of people, this is something that they need to work on. Though not restricted to just management, it is something management needs to be especially aware of since it sets the tone from which others will adapt their behavior.

Being a manager and in charge of people does not give you the right to treat employees like they are second class citizens unworthy of your respect. While the vast majority of managers do not treat employees in this manner, some do and that creates problems for the rest of us. It is important to always remember that our employees are human being just like the rest of us. They want and need the same things as we do even if they are not capable of expressing that to us.

It is also fair to point out that there are employees to do not always treat their managers, or even each other, properly as well. People are different and were raised different. But even though someone might treat us rudely or even be disrespectful does NOT give us the treat to respond in the same manner. We should always take "the high road" and treat people with dignity and respect regardless of how they treat us.

Managers have an additional responsibility as they hold a higher level function within the company and therefore have much higher visibility. While an employee might be able to do something and it go unnoticed, when a manager does the same thing usually everyone notices. Since the behavior of the manager will have a significant effect on how the rest of the staff conducts themselves, the manager must be very careful and aware of how they treat others. It is also important to understand that certain types of behavior might also be against company policy or regional labor laws pertaining to harassment and other behavioral issues.

Treat each other just like you expect or demand others treat you. This is usually the easiest way to figure out how to treat people. Unless you like to be treated poorly by others, this might be the best approach. But always be respectful, do not use coarse or obscene language at any time and never be rude or hostile towards others.

One area that some managers have trouble with is acting like a manager needs to and being authoritative without being condescending at the same time. Being condescending or "talking down" to people is never the right approach as it makes people think that you feel superior to them. Even if you do feel that way, you must never behave in such a way as to convey that to others.

How Do I Do This?

Treat each other with dignity and respect at all times.

If someone treats you badly, still treat them right. If the behavior continues, speak to the employee about it.

Handle all disciplinary issues in private between you and the employee. Never discipline in a group setting.

Respect each other's views and feelings even though you might disagree with them.

Do not make fun of others or use derogatory slang or nicknames for people. Sometimes there is a fine line between kidding and abuse.

Thank about how you would respond before speaking. If you wouldn't like it chances are the other person won't like it either.

Respect each other's commitments and priorities even if they differ from yours.

Don't gossip or talk behind people's backs. It is rude, disrespectful and often inaccurate.

Be Organized

Ok, this one might be a little strange but having good organizational skills in important when it comes to being a good manager. It is important because a manager is usually pulled in 14 different directions at the same time and things can often get lost in the shuffle. Since some of the things manager's have to do directly affect their employees, being organized is critical to the long term success of any manager.

One of the things employee's really dislike, even hate, is when the manager comes to them at the last minute needing something done right away because they forgot about it. So a project that was handed down 3 weeks ago now has to be done in 24 hours often requiring overtime or late nights. Most people understand a late night once in a while but when it is because someone forgot about something until the last minute, that's another story!

Specific tasks such as employee performance and salary reviews need to be completed on time and on schedule so possible salary increases will not be held up or delayed for considerable periods of time. If the manager fails to get things done on time, there can be considerable impact on the employee.

The terms business management and organization are very close to one another. Deadlines are commonplace and most of the time completing one task requires others tasks be completed before hand. Being able to make sure everything gets done and gets done in the proper sequence is critical to a projects long term success.

For example, if you have a big report to do and you need a lot of data to complete that report, it makes sense that you should have the data ready when you intend on writing the report. If you sit down to write the report and don't have the data in front of you, the report is going to be really inaccurate or you will have to wait until you run the data. Common sense would seem to indicate that you run the data the day before you intend on writing the report. That requires a certain amount of planning and organization.

Here are a few more aspects of becoming organized"

Making a List

As much as I hate lists, putting everything down in writing makes it easier to remember things while making it much harder for other things to fall through the cracks. With some projects or tasks being assigned months in advance, it is easy to get caught up in what is happening today while forgetting about what it coming up tomorrow.

I write down everything on a master list and then create a weekly or daily list off the big list. As I complete things I cross them off both the current list and the master list. One great thing about this approach is that you are always seeing everything left on your plate. That helps you keep on top of things almost automatically.

Prioritizing -Managing Deadlines

It is a very lucky manager that doesn't have several projects and commitments going on at the same time. While everything will need to be done on time, the deadlines will all likely be different. That means you have to be able to know what needs to be done NOW and what can be put off until later. Being able to do this is called prioritizing.

For example, if you have two projects to complete and one is due tomorrow and the other 6 months from now, it makes sense to finish the one due tomorrow first and then start on the other one. But if both were due the same day, you would have to decide which is more important or critical to complete first.

Let's say you have two things on your calendar for today. The first is a salary review for an employee and the second is going to Best Buy to buy a pair of headphones. Even though the headphones are on sale, the salary review is more important so you should do that first. Then, buy the headphones on your way home!

Seriously, understand the priority of all the things you have to do make it easier to get more completed on time. Being able to organize multiple projects, events and tasks will take you a long way in making your job easier and less stressful.

As you make your daily or weekly list, take care of the highest priority items first and then move on to the lesser priority things until everything is done.

Sequencing – Project Management

As we said before, some tasks require other tasks be done in a certain order so that you can proceed with the next step.

For example, you have to order materials first before you can start fabrication. You have to do the graphics design before you can print the packaging and so on.

Being able to understand the flow of work and the associated deadlines will help you keep running on schedule and in an orderly fashion. That means less lost time, fewer people waiting around waiting for something to get finished so they can proceed and other delays.

Using a flow chart or pert chart may assist you in managing this type of process but a basic understand of the work flow involved along with good organizational skills is a must.

Scheduling

When it comes to organizing, being able to schedule appropriately is also important. Knowing how much time is needed to perform a certain task, along with the actual amount of time available is critical to proper scheduling.

Most scheduling issues occur when managers allocated too little time or overestimate how much time they really have. They forget the everyday interruptions, last minute tasks, and the always unforeseen things that pop up always it seems at the worst possible times.

The manager should always make sure that he has important tasks and responsibilities completed in advance of deadlines so if unforeseen circumstances do come up, they will have some time to adapt their schedules.

Never shortchange your attention to the needs of your employees. It is alright to limit your availability as long as there are ample opportunities for employees to meet or see you. Allocate time at the beginning of the day when you are likely to have more control. If there are overlapping shifts then try and create an accessible time that works for employees on both shifts.

Review

Even the best laid plans can get blown out of the water when a last minute emergency or request is made. That is why schedules should always have a little bit of free time to help get things back on track. The longer the time period of the schedule, the more free time should be built into it.

Reviewing a schedule should be done once or twice a day to make sure everything is moving along as expected. If it isn't and you find yourself behind, re-evaluate your priorities and alter your schedule according. This might mean moving something to tomorrow or the next day. Do whatever you have to do to create an accurate and achievable schedule.

A Place for Everything

This is one area where just about everyone could stand a bit of improvement. Clutter and dis-organization wastes a ton of hours over the course of a month or year. Searching for papers, reports, tools, data and anything else not only wastes time, it does not impress others who have to wait for you to find something.

When you can't find something, your train of thought is disturbed and you lose your traction and thought process. This will require additional time to review things and get your focus back. That is why it is so important to make sure you have everything you need available to you when you need it.

Create a storage or filing system that you can understand and then use it. Don't let things get out of hand. The last thing you want to deal with is a two foot stack of papers that is going to take you 3 hours you don't have to file. Do it daily. Remember, the larger the pile or the worse the clutter, the easier it is going to be to lose something or cover something up!

A place for everything and everything in its place should be your motto!

How Do I Do This?

Don't wait until the last minute.

Create a system and then follow it! Make a commitment to leave a clean desk every day when you go home!

Buy a daily planner and USE IT!

Create a master list of tasks and responsibilities and use that list to create monthly, weekly or daily lists. Cross off items as you complete them.

Set a personal goal to finish items BEFORE they are due. Create your own deadlines a few days earlier or longer so you never get caught under last minute pressures.

Create policies and procedures that help your employees become organized as well.

Whatever works for you to remind you of upcoming items, use it!

Create "accessible times" where your employees can come and talk to you. This will confine those interruptions to certain times and allow you to work for longer period of time interruption free for the rest of the day. Just make sure the amount of time you dedicate is convenient and long enough.

Share upcoming projects and deadline when you receive them. Do not wait weeks to bring something to the attention of employees and then tell them it must be done tomorrow!

Be Able to Resolve Conflict

Any time you put two or more people in the same office there is bound to be conflict at one time or another. Any time you put customers and employees together you are going to have conflict as well. Since you cannot eliminate conflict it makes sense that a good manager is skilled at resolving conflict and minimizing the effects of it in the workplace.

Over the course of my life I have seen many a teacher or manager tell two fighting people to "just work it out between the two of you" and move on. While that might make sense to some people, it truly is a profoundly stupid bit of advice. After all, people get into a conflict because they disagree with one another about something.

If they cannot work it out to the point where the manager has to get involved, they are most probably way past "working it out between the two of them".

Managers need to be a calm and impartial arbitrator when it comes to handling conflict in the workplace. This conflict can be business related or involve personal conflict that also exists in the office. Clashing personalities, conflicting schedules, workload issues and the workplace environment itself are all prime sources of conflict. How the manager deals with all these things has a dramatic effect on what the long term fallout is going to be.

Good managers understand that the faster conflict is resolved, the less the effects of that conflict will be. It is only when conflict is allowed to continue and escalate that the problem becomes more severe and more costly to resolve. Prompt attention to the situation in the early stages is the best way to handle any kind of conflict.

Resolving conflict involves two very important processes. The first process is the process used to resolve the problem. That means listening to both sides and taking the proper action. The second part of the equation is learning what the source of the conflict was in the first place and then creating processes to eliminate or at least reduce those situations in the future. In other words, trying to learn from our mistakes.

Though entire books have been written on resolving conflict, here are a few things about conflict that every manager should be aware of:

Personality Clash

Just like there are no two snowflakes exactly alike, no two people are exactly alike either. Everyone is different and everyone likes and dislikes different things. That can make working together a challenge at times. Resolving these issues is part of the responsibility of the manager.

The best way of handling these situations is talking things through with the people involved and try to reach a compromise. Failing in that the manager might be forced to make an "executive decision" and decide what is going to happen in the future. This might involve telling one person they have to adjust to different conditions or put up with how things currently are. Or, in some cases it might mean separating the two people or reassigning one or the other.

In some cases, there are people who just like to complain. In that case, it is up to the manager to make sure that one difficult or unreasonable person does not dictate what everyone else has to put up with. A bully in the workplace can be disastrous to overall morale.

Preaching Tolerance

One thing that seems to go by the wayside lately is the ability of people to tolerate anything that is different than their own personal ideals. If anyone acts or looks different, or if they talk different than everyone else, that now creates a problem or friction in the office. The best way to get around these situations is to try and get people to practice a little bit of tolerance in the workplace. We all have to try and get along with others.

Environment Clashes

Along with personality issues and actions, there are environmental issues that sometimes cause problems as well. Some people like it cold and others like it hot. Some people like country music while others like classic rock or show tunes. There is really no perfect answer to this other than to agree with the masses and try to have certain periods of the day when someone gets a little bit of something they like.

Workload Clashes

When someone perceives they are working harder than the others, or when they believe that one or two employees are getting treated differently than the rest of them, this can create a problem.

The best way to deal with this is to make a concerted effort to treat everyone equally and spread the workload equally between all the employees. If the problem still exists you might have to have a meeting or two to talk things out and explain why things are the way they are.

Compromising

The best way to resolve any conflict is to come up with a resolution where everyone gets as much of what they need or want as possible. Instead of looking for a win-lose type of resolution, we should be looking for a win-win solution where everyone leaves or walks away happy.

For example, if someone likes it warmer in the office than everyone else, maybe you switch her desk to be near the heating vent or the window in the summer. If the music in the office is a distraction maybe you allow that person to move further away from the speakers or allow them to wear ear-plugs. Which brings up to the next bullet point.

Thinking Outside the Box

Sometimes the best solutions are the ones no one ever thought of yet. They might appear unconventional or even downright crazy. But if they work, and everyone is happy, who is to say that wasn't the right thing to do?

If someone is really difficult to get along with and complains about everything from the music to the temperature to the cologne or perfume people around them wear, why not consider abandoning company procedure and give her a private office. I doubt if the other employee would mind. They will probably be overjoyed to be rid of her!

Physical Confrontation

Sometimes conflict gets escalated to the point where things become physical. First of all every effort should be made to intervene before things get to this point. But when things do become physical between employees the manager must swift and decisive action. They must separate the employees involved and let everyone understand that physical aggression will never be tolerated for any reason no matter who is the instigator. For other reasons, this should also be stated in the company handbook.

No one deserves to be physically assaulted or abused in the workplace. There are rules and regulations in place to protect employees from this kind of activity. Managers must be aware of these rules and review them from time to time with all employees so that everyone understands the company position on physical violence and abuse.

Resolve in Private

Almost always conflict is best resolved in private. When a manager handles conflict in a public forum or location the people involved might be resistant to back down in the presence of others. When a discussion occurs in private people are usually more willing to get into a conciliatory frame of mind and will be more willing to compromise or admit their role in the situation.

Plus, and this is important, handling any negative matter in public is just the right way to handle things. It is the respectful and dignified way to handle negative situations. It should not be about who looks weaker or stronger but rather what the final result was.

Develop Rules and Procedures

Sometimes conflict occurs when one or more people are confused as to how things are supposed to be done or what the correct procedure might be. The best way to deal with this is to have a written set of rules and procedures to address the most common complaints, disputes or situations. This way when those situations arise, employees can be directed to the company manual to provide the needed information. If that does not do the trick the manager must get involved.

A good manager understands that part of their responsibilities include establishing a good workplace environment and making that environment something that is positive to the majority of the people working in it. That includes handling conflicts properly when they do occur and not ignoring them or hiding in the office and hoping the resolve themselves.

Because they rarely get resolved without outside intervention and mediation.

Be Human

In the movies and in books there is sometimes a stereotyped manager who is ruthless and cold hearted and will do anything and everything to get ahead. He is totally focused on the company and his or her job to the exclusion of everything else. Nothing is more important than closing the deal or making the sale. While that is not a problem in the movies or in books, being that way in real life can make being an employee a living hell.

This one is a little thing that can pay huge dividends to any manager. Since business sometimes has a reputation for being ruthless and impersonal, anything that adds even a little bit of compassion to the workplace can be very important. While this does not mean the manager should become the employee's best friend, it does mean the manager should not hesitate to show a little bit of their "human side".

Contrary to what people might say or believe, showing compassion and being aware of the human, or emotional, side of life is important for any manager. You cannot assume that your employees are available to you 24/7 and that they have nothing else in their lives that is more important than their jobs.

Employees are people and people have families and other aspects of their lives that compete with their job for time and emotions. A good manager understands this and tries to create a work environment that takes employees needs and emotions into consideration.

For example, sometimes workloads can skyrocket due to a sudden increase in sales, a project that is running behind its deadline or some other reason. Manpower might be short and necessitate working a lot of overtime. Sometimes this goes on for too long and employees can become stressed or burned out.

A manager will also understand that there will be times when an employee must take a day off or leave early or come in late for some reason. Important things like attending your child's graduation, visiting a child or close relative who is in the hospital, family deaths or emergencies and other situations where people will need to be accommodated. All of these things must be understood by the manager.

I worked for a manager a long time ago who I never forgot. This manager came in late, left early and took long breaks to go to the gym during the day. But he expected his employees to come in early, work late and to do whatever needed to be done to get things done to the exclusion of everything else. If you had tickets to a show over the weekend and he told you to work that weekend on the Friday before, you had better work. If you asked for a day off for any reason, he would ridicule you and give you a talk about "having the right priorities". If anyone questioned him about anything, his reply would be "If I am committed to this job so should you".

This type of attitude caused the morale in the office to become extremely low. The manager soon became someone who was universally disliked and sometimes made fun of. I should also mention that employee turnover was extremely high. People could just not tolerate that type of work environment for too long. Expectations were ridiculously high and nothing you did was every enough.

A good manager will learn how to balance the needs of the office or business with the needs and limitations of the employees. While a manager must have a human component in their relationships with their employees, they should not carry that so far as becoming friends or drinking buddies outside of work. Going that far opens up other problems.

Instead, a good manager makes decisions that allow their employees to integrate their work responsibilities with the other parts of their lives. That means sometimes altering a work schedule so that one person can spend more time with out of town relatives who are in for a visit or to prepare for a wedding or other event.

It might mean letting someone come in 2 hours earlier and leaving two hours earlier during baseball season so the employee could watch their son play Varsity baseball. Little things like that not only help the employee enjoy their lives more but also strengthen the feelings the employees have for their company and their manager.

Sometimes the manager must say no to certain requests if they create problems for other employees or when they interfere with an important project or deadline. But businesses usually don't have those situations every day or every week. So usually employee needs can be met and employees granted their requests without causing undue hardship for the company. Like I said, it is often a balancing act.

A good manager will always insert a human component in their decisions and assignments. They will understand that people have both physical and emotional limitations. They will understand that all employees need a break or a rest from time to time.

In other words, good managers treat their people like people and not robots or machines.

How Do I Do This?

Make an effort to see your employees as people not just workers.

Always be aware of conditions that might cause employee burnout. Do expect people to come to you to complain. Many employees will be hesitant to do so.

Take the time to know a little bit about your employees. If you have a really large number of employees in your area this may prove difficult. But try and make an effort.

Be pro-active from time to time and do something nice for people who have worked very hard.

Acknowledge an employee who has suffered a problem or loss in their lives. That will mean a lot to the employee. Send flowers or other things from the company during these times.

Be aware of what goes on in the workplace. If you see someone struggling or having a problem, try and help them or at least talk to them. Showing concern for people is something that often means a lot to employees.

Be Honest!

I saved this one for last because it is the one character trait that should be automatic in everyone. Being honest and forthright is the cornerstone for any relationship and the manager / employee relationship is certainly no different. Being honest is the cornerstone around which everything else is built. If a manager is not honest, they lose all credibility.

Managers must be open and honest with their employees at all times. They should never tell someone something just because that is what they think the employee wants to hear. They should be truthful and open in any conversation or correspondence.

Some managers believe that lying or telling people something just to make them happy when they have no intention of keeping their word is an acceptable practice.

Not only is this not an acceptable practice, it just usually makes things worse when the employee or other person finds out the truth later on.

In addition, when a manager lies to anyone, sometimes the reaction of that lie comes down on someone else. For example, if a manager lies to a customer and says he or she will get something that they are not really going to receive, the follow-up call or visit from that customer is likely going to be handled by someone else. That means another employee will have to deal with the original lie and an even angrier customer.

Another reason is that often commitments are made based on lies. For example if a manager tells you that you can have next Wednesday off and you purchase tickets to a show, if you have to work, then you lose the money you paid for the tickets. Or if your manager says he will write you a strong recommendation for a promotion and then never does, that could prevent you from getting the job. For every lie there are repercussions.

Some managers also use lies to avoid taking responsibility. They will make up another story to blame someone else for their mistakes. "No sir, that was not my idea. Bob did that and that is why we are getting sued. I had nothing to do with that."

When a statement like that is made, people now think that Bob is the cause of the problem when, in fact, Bob was doing exactly what the manager told him to do. Now Bob gets the blame and he might not even be aware of it. Bob might lose his job and never know the reason why!

A manager is placed in a position of trust. Employees must trust that their boss is doing things that are correct and they must trust enough in their boss to follow his suggestions without much question. If they need to stop and wonder if the boss is telling the truth this time or not, then everything slows down and may even come to a complete stop.

Sometimes there is also a fine line between telling employees the complete unvarnished truth and shielding them from certain things that are out of their control. In these cases the manager must carefully weigh the pro's and con's and decide which information to share and which information to hold back. This might be a moot point if upper management makes it clear that certain information remain confidential. But the manager must always at least attempt to be fair and honest with all employees.

Sometimes the truth is not an easy thing to say to someone.

It might require telling someone something that is very hurtful or negative in nature and in those times, the best thing the manager can do is deliver the information with tact and compassion. Unfortunately these are the most difficult parts of the role of the manager and it takes time and experience in order to handle them well.

But regardless of the situation, both manager and employee must always be honest with one another and continue to build a bond based on mutual trust. This must continue over time as well. Trust is something that can take years to develop and minutes to destroy. Guard the trust others have in you carefully because once you lose it you may never be able to get it back.

How Do I Do This?

The most obvious piece of advice is to not lie to anyone.

Do not make commitments or promises you cannot keep.

Do not make promises or commitments for others without discussing it with them first.

If you have to say NO to anyone, give them legimate reasons why. Do not lie or make up false reasons.

Take responsibility for your decisions and actions.

Make informed decisions based on fact so if you do make a mistake you will have good reasons behind it. Then you can easily tell the truth and explain your actions.

Never blame someone else for your mistakes or for following your direction.

Create a workplace environment and culture where people will not be afraid to admit their mistakes or errors.

Conclusion

I hope you have learned a few things about what a good manager should represent and how they should interact with their employees. The manager / employee relationship can be a complex one at times but the basis for all of these relationships is based on mutual respect and trust.

The employee and manager do not have to agree with each other on everything and they usually don't. But they still must believe on some level that they have each other's "back" when it comes to what happens in the workplace. With this kind of feeling more gets done, more is accomplished in less time, and workplace stress is low most of the time.

This is not to say that every day will be a walk in the park and everyone will always be happy.

Life just doesn't work that way. But the difference is that when the foundation of a relationship is strong, the little day to day problems and distractions become fewer and of less intensity. Things happen, they are resolved and everyone moves on.

All that being said, it is important to remind both employee and manager that this relationship depends on the actions of BOTH parties. Not 50%-50% but 100%-100%. The best relationships are when both parties want to do their absolute best for the other. This is when the magic happens and everything just goes easier and better.

I have heard from many a manager that they felt taking the time to work with their employees was something they just didn't have time for. While some managers thought their employees were "beneath them" in the company most stated that there was so much to do as a manager that they had no time for building relationships.

If you still feel that way after reading this book, I have two things for you to think about.

First, the time we spend building relationships with employees and treating them with dignity and respect will pay back huge dividends over time and make your life as a manager much easier. Employee turnover will be much less saving you time and resources in training new people. Employees will work harder and product better results for you.

This will help make you look better as a manager at the same time. All of this means that you will have less to do on a daily basis so your life will be less stressful and more rewarding.

The second thing to think about is that you might consider reading this book all the way through from cover to cover again. Stop after every chapter and be honest with yourself. Take the materials and convert it so it directly applies to your position and your situation. Sometimes when you do this, if you are completely honest, you will see your viewpoints shift if even just slightly.

But if you are like the vast majority of managers who read this book, you will have learned a few things and now it's time to take what you have learned and implement it into your management style. Remember that knowledge is a wonderful and powerful tool but it will only have value if you use it.

Made in the USA
Las Vegas, NV
21 April 2024

88974309R00075